The Birth of a State

Sean Price

Chicago, Illinois

Designed by Kimberly R. Miracle and Betsy Wernert
Photo Research by Tracy Cummins
Map on page 30 by Mapping Specialists
Printed by Leo Printing Company

12 11 10 09 08
10 9 8 7 6 5 4 3 2 1

Library of Congress Cataloging-in-Publication Data
Price, Sean.
  The birth of a state : California missions / Sean Price.
      p. cm. -- (American history through primary sources)
  Includes bibliographical references and index.
  ISBN-13: 978-1-4109-2694-4 (hardcover)
  ISBN-13: 978-1-4109-2705-7 (pbk.)
 1. California--History--To 1846--Juvenile literature. 2. Missions, Spanish--California--History-
-Juvenile literature. 3. Spaniards--California--History--Juvenile literature. 4. Indians of North
America--Missions--California--Juvenile literature. I. Title. II. Title: California missions.
  F864.P93 2008
  979.4'01--dc22
                        2007005906

Acknowledgments
The author and publisher are grateful to the following for permission to reproduce copyright
material: Sky Bonillo/Photo Edit **p. 4**; Library of Congress Geography and Map Division **p. 5**;
Lake County Museum/CORBIS **pp. 6, 18–19**; The Granger Collection **p. 7**; The Art Archive /
Navy Historical Service Vincennes France / Dagli Orti **p. 9**; North Wind / North Wind Picture
Archives **p. 11**; Santa Clara University Archives **pp. 12, 13**; Richard Cummins/CORBIS **p. 15**;
Michael Maslan Historic Photographs/CORBIS **p. 16**; David Olsen/Getty Images **p. 17**; Chuck
Pefley / Alamy **p. 21**; Morton Beebe/CORBIS **pp. 22–23**; CORBIS **pp. 24–25**; Phil Klein/
Corbis **p. 26**; Mary Even Picture Library **p. 28**; Everett Collection **p. 29**.

Cover Image of Mission Santa Barbara postcard reproduced with permission of Lake County
Museum/CORBIS.

The publishers would like to thank Isabel Tovar and Nancy Harris for their assistance in the
preparation of this book.

Contents

Spanish California

In the 1500s, Spain ruled a large **empire**. That means it controlled many lands. Spain is in Europe. (See map, page 30). The Spanish paid people to find new lands. These people were called **explorers**. One of them was Christopher Columbus. He was one of the first Europeans of his time to find America. The year was 1492.

Spanish explorer Juan Rodriguez Cabrillo reached California in 1542.

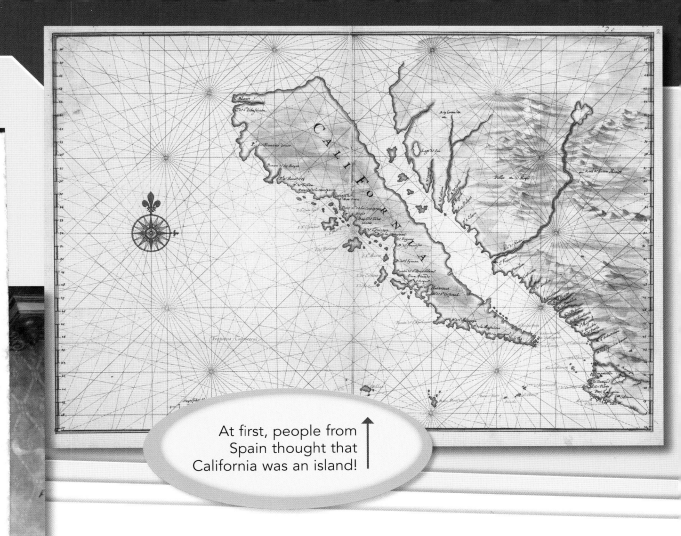

At first, people from Spain thought that California was an island! ↑

Later explorers found out more about America. They discovered the size of America. One of these explorers was Juan Rodriguez Cabrillo. In 1542, he became the first person from Europe to reach California. Cabrillo claimed California for Spain. Many Native Americans already lived in California then. But they called the land by other names.

Spain did little with California at first. Few Spanish people wanted to live there. It was too far from Spain. So the Spanish did not learn much about the area. For many years, they believed California was an island.

Starting the missions

In the 1700s, the countries of Russia and Great Britain sent explorers to California. They wanted to take the area away from Spain. They wanted any wealth the area might have.

Father Junípero Serra

Father Junípero Serra set up the first missions in California. He was a Catholic priest. Serra began his work in 1769. His health was weak. Still, Serra traveled a lot. He started nine missions before dying in 1784.

Spain planned to stop this. It set up **missions** in California. Missions were like small villages. Their top job was to spread the **Roman Catholic** faith. A Roman Catholic is a type of Christian. Catholics see the Pope as their leader.

Catholic priests worked as **missionaries**. Missionaries spread the Catholic faith to Native Americans. They also ran missions. All the missions were named after angels or **saints**. Saints are very holy people.

Soldiers helped Spanish priests set up missions. ↓

The first Californians

The Spanish were not the first people in California. The area already had about 150,000 Native Americans. They had lived there a long time. These Native Americans belonged to many **tribes**, or groups. They spoke different languages.

Most hunted and fished for their food. They also gathered nuts, fruits, and seeds. Native Americans had no written language. But they were good at making tools. They also enjoyed group dances. They had hunting dances. There was also a war dance. There were many other dances, too.

Native Americans were often forced to stay in the **missions**. They could not leave if they wanted to. Because of this, many Native Americans did not like the missions. Some burned missions. They killed **missionaries**. In time, some Native Americans accepted the missions. Yet many never did.

Native American religions

Native Americans already had their own beliefs. Most were tied closely to nature. Some believed that things like water or animals were spirits. But most of these beliefs have been lost. That is because missionaries forced many Native Americans to change their beliefs.

tribe   group of people who live and work together

Dance was important to California's Native Americans.

Life at a Mission

The Spanish set up **missions** in California. They did it between 1769 and 1823. There were 21 missions in all. They were placed near a road. The road was called El Camino Real. That means the King's Highway. It was California's first major road.

People could go from one mission to the next by horse. This took about a day. **Roman Catholic** priests ran each mission. Spanish soldiers guarded them. The missions were also home to **neophytes**. These were Native Americans who became Catholics.

Canticle of Dawn

Work at a mission began at sunrise. People sang this song each morning. It was called **Canticle** of Dawn. A canticle is a type of song. It was a song to Mary. Mary was the mother of Jesus.

Now comes the dawn

Brightening to the day

Hail, Mary Hail,

Let us all say ...

neophytes   Native Americans who became Catholics.
canticle   type of song

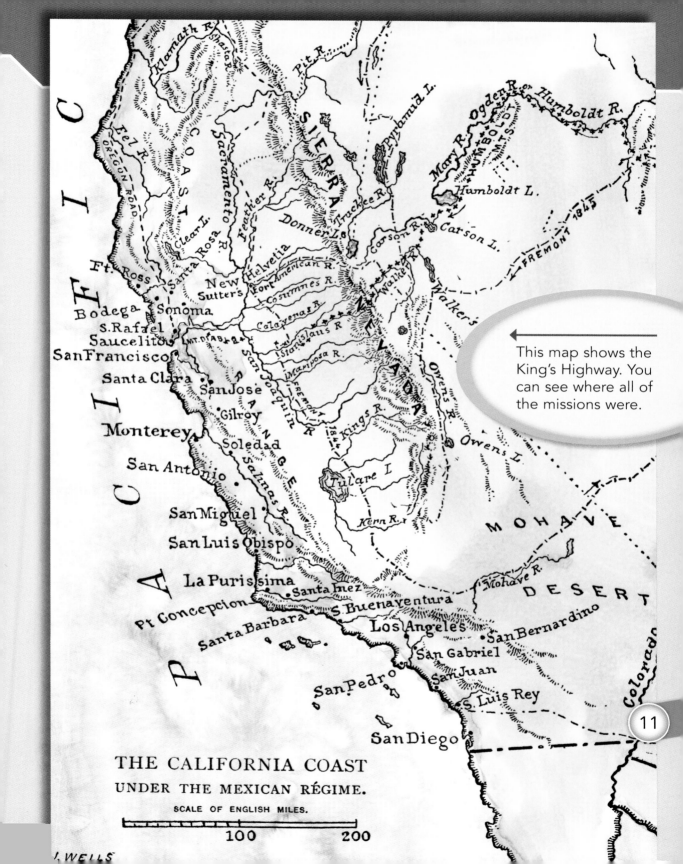

This map shows the King's Highway. You can see where all of the missions were.

THE CALIFORNIA COAST
UNDER THE MEXICAN RÉGIME.

SCALE OF ENGLISH MILES.

100   200

Provincia dela Nueva California

Resumen general q.e manifiesta el estado en q.e se hallan los nuevos establecimientos de esta Provincia, y expresa los Presidios y Misiones de Indios, y Pueblos de Gente de razon de q.e se componen: el numero de sus habitantes de ambos sexos inclusos los Parbulos. Cabezas de Ganado de toda especie q.e poseen, y Fanegas de Granos q.e ultimamente cosecharon, relacionandose por notas lo demas concerniente al conocimiento de sus actuales circunstancias hasta fin de Diciembre de 1824.

Nombres de las Poblaciones	Gente de razon e Indios					Ganado Mayor				Idem menor			Fanegas ultimam.te cosechadas					Total de Fanegas
	Hombres	Mugeres	Niños	Niñas	Total	Vacuno	Caballar	Mular	Corral	De Lana	De Pelo	De Cerda	Trigo	Maiz	Frijol	Cevada	Varias legumbres	
													20.	214.	25.	144.	800.	210.	13
													40.	237.	380.	5.	567.	38.	3
Presidio de Monterey	127.	99.	103.	77.	406.	2000.	508.	20.		5.400.	16.	35.	1.018.		36.	243.	448.	52.	1
Mision de San Carlos	125.	105.	38.	35.	306.	832.	808.	42.	2.	570.		28.	77.	1.355.	90.	44.	308.	52.	11
Idem. de S.n Juan Bautista	523.	441.	108.	149.	1221.	4200.	950.	50.	1.	9000.		5.	100.	1.200.	12.	6.	12.	11.	1
Y.d de N.S de la Soledad	281.	140.	49.	42.	512.	6100.	1070.	34.	2.	9000.			20.	1.060.		30.		20.	
Y.d de San Antonio	435.	245.	60.	66.	806.	4092.	1500.	76.	20.	11.024.									
Y.d de San Miguel	408.	361.	70.	65.	904.	7700.	1520.	160.	60.	5000.									
Y.d de San Luis Obispo	264.	151.	12.	11.	438.					4366.				504.	45.	11.	103.	120.	
Pueblo de S.n Jose de Guadalupe					228.								5.	1.300.	190.	40.	700.	13.	
Pres. de San Francisco	80.	52.	49.	40.	265.	2521.	262.	23.		3000.				500.	200.	6.			
Mision de Ydem	156.	86.	16.	7.	265.	900.	280.	4.		4000.			25.	135.	200.	108.	252.	162.	
Asistencia de S. Rafael	386.	377.	90.	86.	939.	1100.	450.	16.		13.500.				1.318.	375.	572.	371.	126.	
Mis.n de S.n Fran.co Solano	365.	254.	79.	74.	692.	7000.	800.	22.		6.000.				2.500.	40.	40.	150.	29.	
Y.d de Santa Clara	752.	528.	95.	75.	461.	3000.	416.	26.		15.000.									
Ydem de Santa Cruz	244.	162.	31.	1.	1806.	3000.	650.	15.											
	371.	694.	112.	129.	99.								100.	870.	102.	30.	200.		
	15.	91.	10.	15.	582.			200.		2.500.			80.		10.	12.		300.	
				132.	108.	1200.	500.	100.		2.400.									
				78.	923.	5800.	5600.	100.											
				66.	516.					3.500.									
					908.	4000.	250.	80.		3.500.	15.	70.							
					957.	4000.	280.	100.	14.										
				170.	178.	837.													
					1829.	8536.	845.	330.	7.	19.000.	235.	40.							
Pres. de S.n Diego	805.	592.	223.	205.	1644.	13.304.	510.	94.		7.100.	14.	20.							
Mision de Ydem	638.	562.	220.	224.	98.	1060.	10.000.	370.	82.	4.500.	40.								
Ydem de San Gabriel	461.	391.	107.		2767.	14.556.	1305.	142.	4.	21.507.	656.								
Y.d de S.n Juan Capistrano	1121.	1050.	321.	272.															
Ydem de S. Luis Rey						127.329.	20.061.	1938.	110.	163.403.	1166.	10.							
Totales																			

Notas

1.a ... Entre las Misiones q.e preceden se han verificado en el presente año 480. Matrimonios. ... Neofitos ya congregados, y 929. Gentiles é hijos de estos, q.e hacen el numero de 1625. los bautizados. Se han Bautizado 172. y h... todo de Indios. Entre los de razon se han celebrado 30. Matrimonios. ... en este ... de 103. Almas.

2.a ... Reunido el numero de 696. q.e son los nacidos en las Misiones hijos de los ... los 1447. q.e han fallecido. Resulta la perdida real y efectiva de 518. Indios.

3.a ... Almas delos Ganados anotados poseen los Vecinos algun numero de Reses, y Caba... anteriores ha causado en el presente mucha mortandad de Ganados en los Campos delas Mision... ...imo en los Presidios de Monterey, y San Francisco en donde no han quedado de Cue... ...n el de San Diego ninguna q.e se necesita reponer este, y ... ...lo que se executará con lo...

Missions kept records of births, marriages, and deaths.

The mission community

Missions could create strong **communities**. They were communities of **neophytes** and priests. A community is a group of people with close ties.

Many people had homes near the mission lands. These homes were **ranchos**. Ranchos is the Spanish word for *ranches*. People raised cattle on ranchos. They also raised pigs and sheep. Missions raised cattle as well. They also grew crops. People on the ranchos attended the mission churches.

Mission churches allowed people to pray and sing together. Weddings took place at mission churches. So did funerals.

Music played a big role in mission services.

Sitting in church

Today, people sit on **pews** (benches) in church. But back then, seats were not used. People sat on the floor. Men and boys sat on one side. Women and girls sat on another.

An End and a Beginning

The **missions** were built by Native Americans. These workers made the buildings. They made the furniture. They often decorated the church. They made beautiful designs. Their artwork still exists at the Mission San Miguel.

Not all Native Americans liked the missions. Many saw work there as **slavery**. A slave is owned by someone else. Slaves have no freedom. **Neophytes** often tried to leave missions. They wanted to rejoin their **tribes**. Spanish soldiers hunted them down. They brought them back to the missions.

Mexico had been ruled by Spain. (See map, pg. 30.) In 1821, Mexico became **independent** (free) of Spain. Mexico took control of California. Many Mexicans did not like the missions. They were seen as part of Spain's control. They divided mission lands among many people.

Without land, missions could not support themselves. This forced priests to leave. By 1845, most of the missions had shut down. Neophytes had nowhere to go. Many worked as slaves for the new owners of the old mission land.

Rebuilding the missions

In 1848, the U.S. defeated Mexico in a war. Americans now had control of California. In 1850, California became a state. In 1863, all of the **missions** were returned to the Catholic Church.

The missions faced many problems. Priests had little money. They could not take care of missions. Buildings began to crumble. Most were made with **adobe**. Adobe is a type of dirt or clay. The adobe washed off in the rain. Few buildings could be repaired. California has strong earthquakes as well. The earthquakes did a lot of damage.

This San Diego mission fell into ruin.

This is the same mission rebuilt. Many other missions were rebuilt, too.

Also, people took bricks and roof tiles from the old missions. They used them to build their own houses.

By 1880, most missions were in ruins. They were falling apart. Luckily, people in California took an interest in these beautiful buildings. They began to wonder about the history of their state. Groups formed to **restore** (repair) the missions. It took many years to fix and rebuild them.

18

converted   changed beliefs

Mission Images

Mission Santa Barbara is called the "Queen of the Missions." It was large and rich. It never closed down like the other missions. Mission Santa Barbara began in 1786. Catholic priests have run it ever since.

Mission Santa Barbara consisted of many buildings. The buildings formed a box. The church was the largest building. The others made long rows. Some were homes for priests. Others were workshops and storerooms.

More than 1,000 Native Americans helped build Mission Santa Barbara. They worked in its shops and fields. These Native Americans were **neophytes**. They had **converted** (changed their beliefs) to the Catholic Church. The Native Americans lived at the mission, too.

The first church at Mission Santa Barbara was just a small hut. But the mission grew. Bigger buildings were needed. The church was rebuilt four times. The church seen today was not built until 1820. That was nearly 35 years after the mission started.

Mission Santa Barbara had many rich lands.

La Purísima Concepcíon

Missions got some money from Spain. But they had to support themselves. They did this by creating goods that were useful. They sold or traded these goods to people. Missions also had to raise their own food. They did that by farming. They did it by raising cattle and sheep.

Mission La Purísima Concepcíon was famous for the things it made. Native Americans there became skilled workers. Missions had many animal hides. They came from the cattle and the sheep. Native American workers made leather from the hides. They made saddles. They made leather jackets.

The mission was also known for its blankets. Workers created them on big **looms**. A loom is a machine that weaves cloth. Native Americans also wove fine baskets. They did that by hand. Some were woven tightly. They could even hold water! People paid the mission to buy these items. Sadly, very few examples of them remain.

Mission La Purísima was famous for leather goods, like saddles.

loom   machine that weaves cloth

Disease killed many at
Mission San Francisco. ↓

Mission San Francisco de Asís

Some **missions** faced hard times. The Mission San Francisco de Asís was one of them.

The mission had many Native American **neophytes**. But **disease** (illness) struck Mission San Francisco hard. Many Native Americans there died. Measles killed most of them. Measles is a disease.

Spanish people brought these diseases. The illnesses killed many Spanish people, as well. In 1769, Spain sent 219 people to set up Mission San Diego. Sickness killed half of them. But diseases hurt far more Native Americans. They had never seen illnesses like measles. Their bodies had no natural protection.

Little survives of Mission San Francisco de Asís. There is only the church and **cemetery** (burial ground). More than 5,000 Native Americans are buried there.

The birth of cities

The city of San Francisco gets its name from this mission. The mission had problems. But its name stuck. Other California cities began as missions. They include San Diego and Santa Barbara.

23

Mission San Juan Capistrano

Mission San Juan Capistrano is often called the "Jewel of the Missions." It has always been one of the most beautiful. It was built in 1776.

In 1796, **neophytes** began building the "Great Stone Church." The church was five stories high. It was one of the nicest in California. Sadly, an earthquake destroyed it in 1812. The mission could not rebuild it. Then in 1833, Mexico took away Mission San Juan's lands. The mission closed.

The U.S. returned it to the Catholic Church in 1865. Over time, priests planted gardens. They fixed many buildings but not all of them. Today, San Juan Capistrano is popular with tourists. They travel to visit the mission.

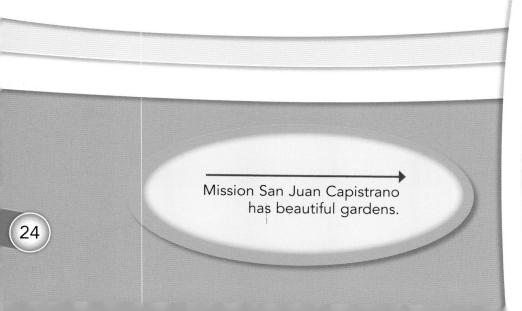

Mission San Juan Capistrano has beautiful gardens.

Swallows of Capistrano

Each March, swallows **migrate** (travel) to San Juan Capistrano. They build nests in the Stone Church ruins. The birds fly from Argentina. That is 7,500 miles away! They come because it is warmer in California. The birds fly back to Argentina each fall.

⬆ This is Mission San
Miguel Arcángel after

Mission San Miguel Arcángel

A 2003 earthquake rattled **Mission** San Miguel Arcángel. The old church was badly damaged. It was popular with tourists. But now it is unsafe to go inside.

Money is needed to fix the church. Mission San Miguel does not have enough. Famous artwork can be found on its walls. The paintings were done by Spanish and Native American artists. Few missions still have such fine art. Repairs like this are a challenge for all missions. Their buildings need to be taken care of.

Also, many mission **relics** are in danger. Relics are old items. Some missions still have the clothes worn by Spanish priests. Others have wooden tools and crosses. These relics must be cared for in special ways. Again, that costs money. Raising the money is hard. But people think it is important. Missions are an important part of California history.

Missions vs. Disneyland

Missions are California's second-biggest tourist attraction. Only Disneyland draws more people.

Ramona

In the 1880s, most **missions** were falling apart. That changed thanks in part to a **novel**. The made-up story was called *Ramona*. It was written by Helen Hunt Jackson in 1884. In the book, Ramona is a half Native-American girl. She lives near a mission. She falls in love with a boy. But they have a tough life together. People try to split them up.

Helen Hunt Jackson wrote the novel *Ramona*.

novel	book with a made-up story
inspire	give people the idea to do something
pageant	show

INSPIRATION PICTURES, INC. & EDWIN CAREWE PRESENT

DOLORES DEL RIO

IN "RAMONA"

HELEN HUNT JACKSON'S AMERICAN LOVE CLASSIC

AN EDWIN CAREWE PRODUCTION

UNITED ARTISTS PICTURE

SCREEN PLAY BY FINIS FOX

SUPPORTED BY
WARNER BAXTER
VERA LEWIS
ROLAND DREW
MICHAEL VISAROFF

↑ *Ramona* inspired many plays and movies.

Jackson's novel was very popular. It got Americans interested in California's past. Suddenly, people wanted to save the missions. They even built homes that looked like missions. These homes are called "Spanish mission" style.

Ramona is still read today. The book **inspired** (gave ideas to) people. They wrote movies and songs based on *Ramona*. Today, there is still a Ramona **Pageant**. It is a giant play held near the city of Los Angeles each spring. The pageant started in 1923. It is the longest-running outdoor play in the United States.

Glossary

adobe type of dirt or clay used to build buildings

canticle type of song

cemetery burial ground

community group of people with close ties

converted changed beliefs

disease illness

empire large area controlled by one country

explorer somebody who seeks new places

independent to be free

inspire give people the idea to do something

loom machine that weaves cloth

migrate travel

mission place that tries to spread a religious belief

missionary someone who spreads a religious message

neophytes Native Americans who became Catholics

novel book with a made-up story

pageant show

pew bench-like seat in a church

rancho Spanish word for "ranch"

relic old object

restore rebuild and fix up

Roman Catholic type of Christian

saints holy people

slavery being owned by someone else

tribe group of people who live and work together

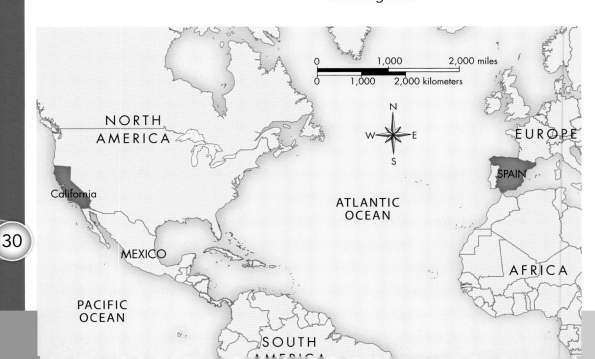

Want to Know More?

Books to read

- Ditchfield, Christin. *Spanish Missions*. New York: Children's Press, 2006.
- Isaacs, Sally Senzell. *Life in a California Mission*. Chicago: Heinemann: 2001
- Heinrichs, Ann. *The California Missions*. Mankato MN: Capstone, 2002.

Websites

- www.lapurisimamission.org
  Learn about mission life at this reconstructed mission. It is now a state park.
- www.parks.ca.gov/pages/479/files/missionsfsolano.htm
  Take a virtual tour of the Mission San Francisco de Solano.

Places to visit

- **La Purísima Mission State Historic Park**
  2295 Purisima Road, Lompac, CA 93436 (805) 733-3713
- **Mission San Juan Capistrano**
  26801 Ortega Highway, San Juan Capistrano, CA 92675 (949) 234-1300

Read **Route 66: America's Road** to find out about this historic road and the many sites along it.

Read **Strike It Rich in Cripple Creek: Gold Rush** to find out why people rushed to the West during the mid-1800s.

Index